Christopher Rouse

Mime

for Snare Drum

Archive Edition

HENDON MUSIC

DISTRIBUTED BY

HAL•LEONARD®
CORPORATION
7777 W. BLUEMOUND RD. P.O. BOX 13819 MILWAUKEE, WI 53213

www.boosey.com
www.halleonard.com

Mime

Pittsford, New York

DeoGratias
June 14, 1997